Contents

My body

My body can **curl** and **stretch**.

4

My body can **twist** and **turn**.

My head

Curly hair

My brain is in here!

My eyes

My eyes can wink or blink.

My eyes can stare or peep.

9

My mouth

tongue

11

My arms

My arms have elbows that bend.

elbow

I can hug my mum with my arms.

13

My hands

My hands can wave goodbye.

My fingers and thumb

My fingers and thumb can help me count

1 2 3 4 5

16

My legs

My legs have knees that bend.

My legs help me
climb and swing.

19

My feet

My feet can kick a ball.

20

My toes

My toes can stretch and wriggle.

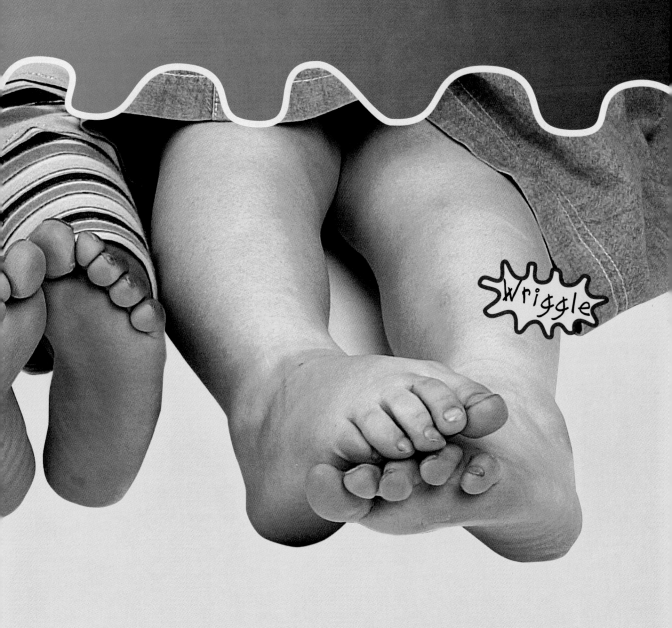

Index

The end

Notes for adults

This series supports the child's knowledge and understanding of their world, in particular their personal, social and emotional development area. The following Early Learning Goals are relevant to the series:
• respond to significant experiences, showing a range of feelings when appropriate
• have a developing awareness of their own needs, views and feelings and be sensitive to the needs and feelings of others
• have a developing respect for their own cultures and beliefs and those of other people.

Each book explores a range of different experiences, many of which will be familiar to the child. There is plenty of opportunity for the child to compare and contrast their own experiences with those of the children depicted in the book. This can be encouraged by asking open-ended questions like: What shape can you make with your hands? Or how has your body changed since you were a tiny baby?

The series will help the child extend their vocabulary. Some words related to **Our Bodies** could include naming other body parts like *nostrils*, *gums*, *wrist*, *ankle*, *knuckles*, *heel* and *instep* and alternative verbs for movement like *pat*, *clap*, *shake*, *leap*, *squeeze*, *point*, *throw*, *catch* and *balance*.

The following additional information about our bodies may be of interest: Movement of different parts of the body is related to the different kinds of joints. Some joints move in only one direction like the elbow and knee. Other joints, like the one at the base of the thumb, allow for circular movement, as do the shoulder joint and the ankle and wrist joints.

Follow-up activities
The child can draw pictures of different figures and see how many different parts of the body can be included. Play 'Simon Says' touching less familiar parts like calf, shin, forehead and palm. Make up alternative verses for 'Head, shoulders, knees and toes'.